HIST

GOLD

by Kelly Gaffney

raintree

a Capstone company — publishers for children

Engage Literacy is published in the UK by Raintree.
Raintree is an imprint of Capstone Global Library Limited, a company incorporated in England and Wales having its registered office at 264 Banbury Road, Oxford, OX2 7DY — Registered company number: 6695582

www.raintree.co.uk

10 9 8 7 6 5 4 3 2 1
Printed and bound in China.

History of Gold
ISBN: 978-1-4747-1787-8

Capstone Press: Capstone, 12, 22; Corbis: Stefano Bianchetti, left 20; Getty Images: Bloomberg, (worker) bottom right 30, George Eastman House, (miners) top 25, Majority World, (miners) top left 30, Robert Gubbins, (panning) bottom 17; iStockphoto: Pgiam, (astronaut) top 7; Library of Congress: Miscellaneous Items in High Demand, (miners) top 23; Newscom: Yuri Smityuk/TASS, 31; Shutterstock: Allgusak, (metal background) design element throughout, Andrey N Bannov, (gold vein) bottom 17, ArtMari, (volcano) modified 14-15, 16, Baloncici, (bars) cover , Bloomua, (phones) top 8, Chones, (trophy) middle 10, Civdis, (building) bottom right 7, cowardlion, (flute) bottom 9, DinoZ, (gold plate) design elemement throughout, Eunika Sopotnicka, (machine) bottom 20-21, Gilmanshin, (electric plate) design element throughout, Isuaneye, (girl) top 21, JaRaKa, (jeans) side 25, Jason Benz Bennee, 27, Jeffrey B. Banke, 18, Jose Ignacio Soto, (mask) 5, jps, (coins) 1, 4, 5, Julia Reschke, (gold nugget) middle 4, junrong, (machine) top right 30, kojihirano, 13, Kuznetcov_Konstantin, (miner left 28, Merkushev Vasiliy, (water cycle) modified 14-15, 16, Mik Lav, (window) top 11, ninanaina, (gold leaf background) cover, Oleksiy Mark, (computer) top 8, optimarc, (gold nuggets) design element throughout, pan_kung, 6, Roman Bodnarchuk, (gold nugget) middle 17 backcover, schankz, (teeth) bottom 11, seaskylab, (dragon) bottom 10, Serhii Neznamov, (miner) right 29, Steve Lovegrove, 26, Taigi, (teapot) bottom 8, vesna cvorovic, (rings) top 9, waniuszka, (mine shaft) 28-29; Wikimedia: Alchemist-hp, (crystal) top right 17, Pinethicket, 19, Skeezix1000, 24, Woodside, H.J, (camp) bottom 23

CONTENTS

PRECIOUS GOLD

Gold is a *precious*, or valuable, metal. People have searched for gold since long ago. It has been used to make beautiful things, such as jewellery and statues. It has also been made into coins and used as money. Even today, gold is very valuable.

WHY IS GOLD SPECIAL?

Gold is special for a lot of reasons. It is a beautiful yellow colour and is one of the world's shiniest metals. Pieces of gold must have looked amazing when they were first discovered.

Gold is a soft metal, so it can be easily made into different shapes. People long ago were able to work with gold using very simple tools. This may be another reason why gold jewellery was popular thousands of years ago.

People can carve designs into gold by hand.

Gold can be made so thin that you can see through it. A very thin layer of gold lets some light through but *reflects*, or throws back, red and yellow light. Therefore, a thin layer of gold can be used to reflect the sun's harmful rays because they bounce back again. This has made gold very useful for protecting *astronauts* and their supplies from the sun.

Windows on very tall buildings often have a thin layer of gold on them, too. This helps to keep the buildings cool.

Gold can be stretched into a thin wire without breaking. *Electricity* travels very well through gold. This is why many electrical products, such as mobile phones and computers, use gold wire.

FACT: Did you know that gold wire is used in televisions, mobile phones and computers?

This teapot is made of silver, but it looks black because it is tarnished.

Gold does not rust or *tarnish*. Some metals, such as silver, turn black if they are not polished. Other metals, such as iron, rust.

Gold can be easily melted and blended with other metals.

These wedding rings are made of white gold.

A mixture of metals is called an *alloy*. Gold alloys are harder and hold their shape better than pure gold.

White gold is made when gold is mixed with another metal, such as nickel.

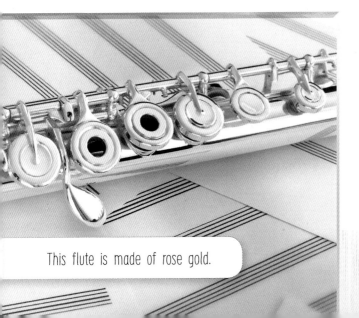

This flute is made of rose gold.

Rose gold is made when gold is mixed with another metal called copper.

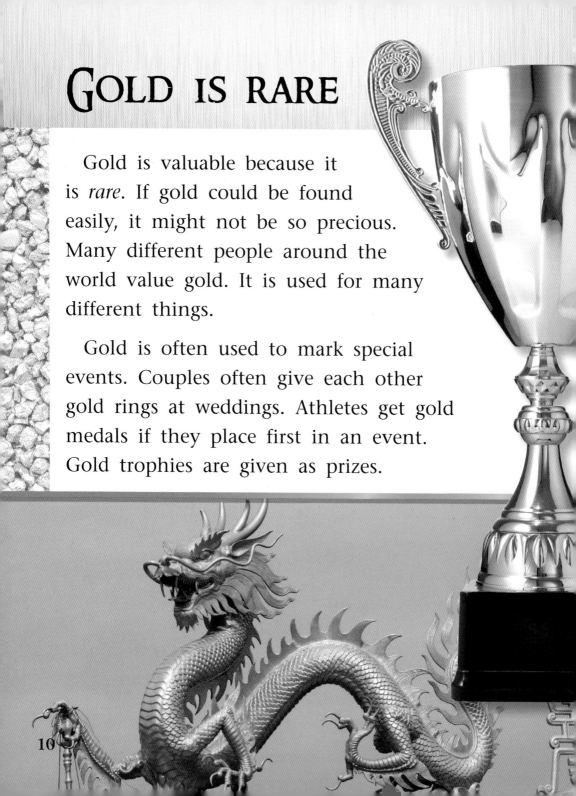

GOLD IS RARE

Gold is valuable because it is *rare*. If gold could be found easily, it might not be so precious. Many different people around the world value gold. It is used for many different things.

Gold is often used to mark special events. Couples often give each other gold rings at weddings. Athletes get gold medals if they place first in an event. Gold trophies are given as prizes.

Gold has many other uses, too. Red glass is made using gold.

Gold has even been used by dentists to make fillings for teeth. It is easy to shape and can last in the mouth for many years.

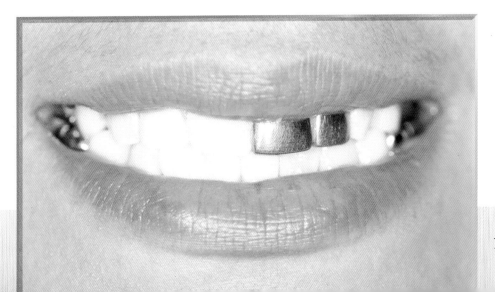

WHERE IS GOLD FOUND?

Gold can be found in places all over the world. The biggest producers of gold are the countries of China, Australia, and the United States.

Gold is usually only *mined*, or dug up, where there are large amounts of it in a small area.

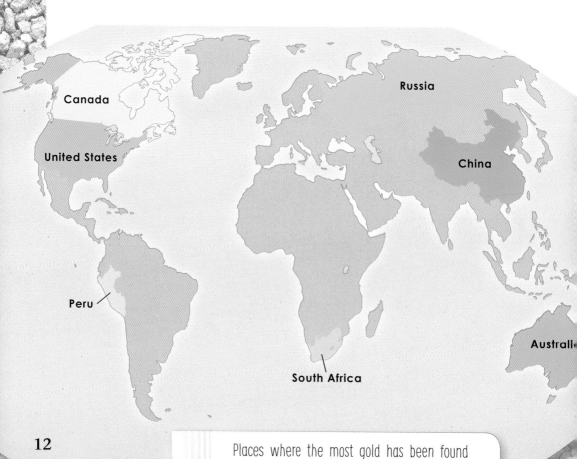

Places where the most gold has been found

FACT: There is a tiny amount of gold in most rocks. There is also gold in sea water. But it costs too much money to get the gold from sea water.

GOLD DEPOSITS

A large amount of gold found in one area is called a *deposit*. There are two different kinds of gold deposits. One is called a *lode deposit*, and the other is called a *placer deposit*.

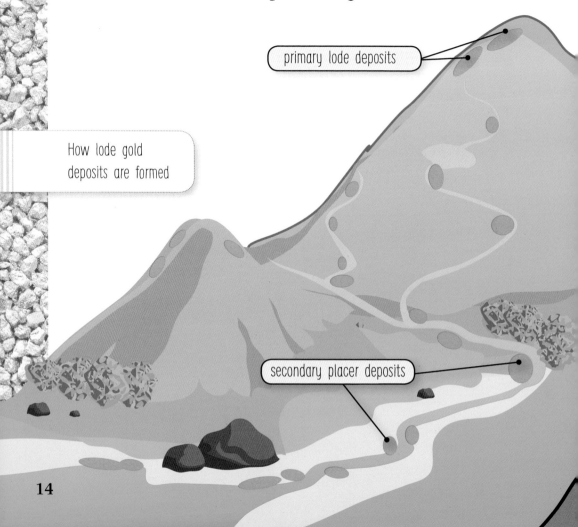

primary lode deposits

How lode gold deposits are formed

secondary placer deposits

Lode deposits are made when very hot water pushes up from deep below the ground. The water melts the gold and carries it up to the Earth's surface. Once the water has cooled, the gold becomes hard again.

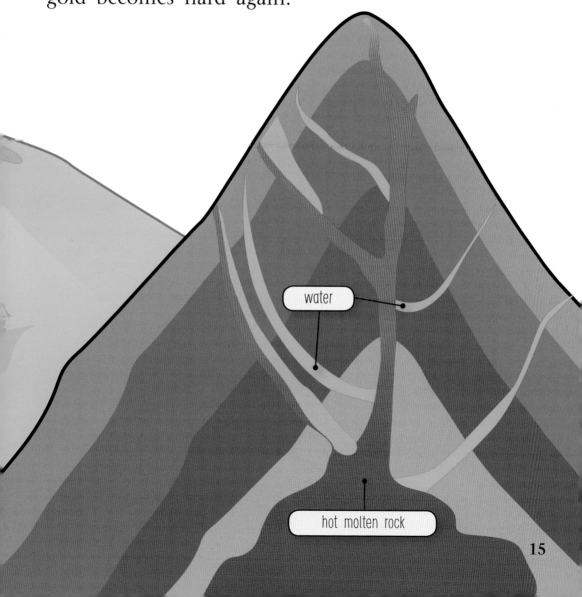

water

hot molten rock

Placer deposits come from lode deposits. Lode deposits can be worn away over time by the wind and the rain. Little bits of gold get washed down streams. The heavy gold bits sink down into the gravel and get stuck behind rocks. Over time, gold may be covered by soil or rocks. These deposits are called placer deposits.

How placer gold deposits are formed

Primary lode deposits are worn away.

Pieces of gold wash down into streams where they sink or stick behind rocks.

Gold can be found in different shapes. It can look like a rock. This is called a gold nugget.

It can also be found in the cracks in a rock. This is called a vein of gold.

Deposits of gold are soft, so they can be dented and scratched by other rocks. This can change the shape of the gold by bending or twisting it.

How can gold be found?

Removing gold from the ground is called mining. The way the gold is mined depends on the type of gold and where people are looking for it.

Shallow gold can be found near rivers and streams. People can use pans and shovels to find this gold. Soil and gravel are dug out from streams and swirled around in a pan. The gold is heavier than soil, so it sinks to the bottom of the pan.

In the past, miners also used wooden boxes called rockers to find shallow gold. They dug up soil and gravel from the bottom of streams. Then they put it into the rocker and added water. The water and the rocking helped to separate the gold from the soil and gravel.

Gold that is deeper underground is harder to find. In the past, miners dug lots of tunnels to reach this gold. These tunnels were called *mine shafts*.

The mine shafts were made stronger with wood to stop the walls from caving in. The rocks and soil that were taken out of the mine shafts were checked carefully for any sign of gold.

Miners in the past made tunnels to search for gold underground.

Today, big mining companies or businesses find most of the gold. These companies use scientists who know a lot about rocks to find places where there might be large amounts of gold. The scientists are called *geologists*. They make maps to show what kind of rocks can be found in an area. The company then drills into the ground to see what sort of rock is beneath the surface.

Now mining companies use scientists and machines to find and remove gold.

GOLD RUSHES

A "gold rush" happens when lots of people move to a place where gold has been found. In the 1800s, there were gold rushes in the countries of Australia, Canada, and the United States. They were also in New Zealand and part of South Africa.

People came from all over the world to look for gold. Large cities of tents seemed to spring up overnight. People left their homes, jobs and sometimes their families, hoping to become rich.

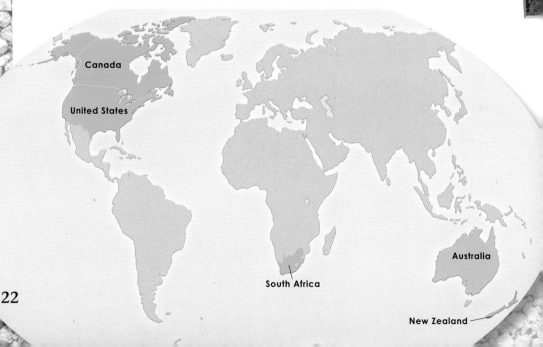

Miners work in the goldfields in California, USA.

Some of these places became *deserted* after a year or two. Deserted towns were known as "ghost towns." Other places kept growing after the gold rush ended.

This tent city was set up during the Klondike Gold Rush in Canada.

Gold rushes caused lots of problems. Businesses found it hard to keep their workers because so many people were leaving for the goldfields. Farmers couldn't get people to work on their farms. Sailors left their ships. Teachers even left their classrooms. Nearly everyone wanted to become rich by finding gold.

Life on the goldfields was hard. Goldfields were dirty places. Fresh food and clean water were hard to find. Many people became sick.

Many people line up to buy miners' licences.

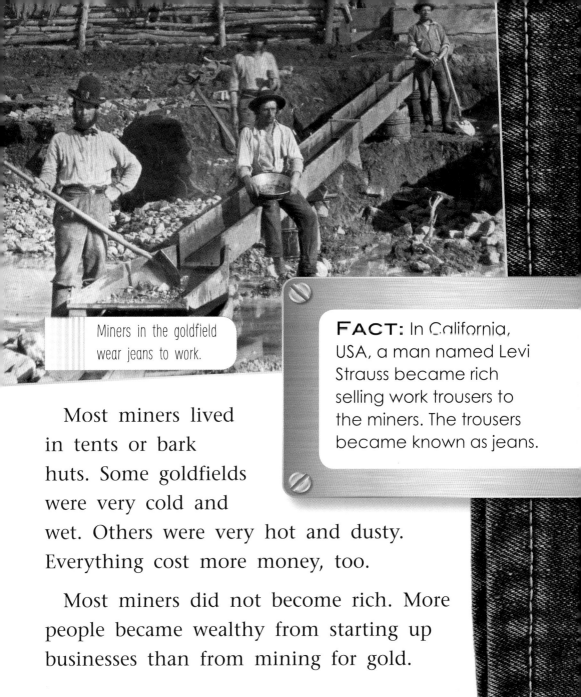

Miners in the goldfield wear jeans to work.

FACT: In California, USA, a man named Levi Strauss became rich selling work trousers to the miners. The trousers became known as jeans.

Most miners lived in tents or bark huts. Some goldfields were very cold and wet. Others were very hot and dusty. Everything cost more money, too.

Most miners did not become rich. More people became wealthy from starting up businesses than from mining for gold.

GOLD MINING TODAY

These days, big mining companies use different types of mines to find gold.

In some places, huge amounts of rock and soil are dug out of the ground. This type of mine is called an *open-cut mine*. Enormous lorries and digging machines remove the soil and rock that is on top of the gold.

After this soil and rock are taken away, the rocks containing gold can be mined.

Large lorries have to drive the rock and soil out of an open-cut mine to make the hole wider and deeper.

In other places, the gold mining takes place deep underground. Mine shafts are dug deep into the ground.

Some of these tunnels are used to take the miners down to the place where gold is being mined.

Today, miners use controls to run machines for digging and carrying out gold.

Many tunnels are drilled deep underground.

Other shafts are used to remove all the rock that the miners dig up. Some of this rock contains gold, but most of it does not. All the equipment needed by the miners comes in and out of the mine through tunnels. These shafts are also needed to get fresh air to the men and women working in the mine.

This miner is using a lift to go down into a mine shaft.

Miners set explosives.

Machines are used to remove rock and gold.

FACT: In some underground mines, the rocks are very hot. Ice is pumped though big pipes to try to keep the air cool.

Chemicals separate gold from rock.

Explosives are used to blow up sections of rock so that they can be removed from the mine. Once the rock comes out of the mine, it is crushed. Then, a *chemical* is used to remove the gold.

It takes a lot of work to find even a little bit of gold. That is why it is so special. Perhaps you can pan for gold one day!

GLOSSARY

alloy a mixture of metals

astronaut person who travels in space

chemical substance or material

deposit natural layer of rock, sand, or minerals found in the ground

deserted everyone has left

electricity natural force that can be used to make light and heat or to make machines work

geologist scientist who studies rocks

lode deposit gold pushed up to the Earth's surface by hot water

mine to dig up

mine shaft tunnel in the ground where metal is dug up

open-cut mine large areas of soil removed from on top of gold or other metals

placer deposit gold carried to another area in river water

precious very special or valuable

rare hard to find

reflect to throw back (light)

shallow not deep

tarnish to reduce or change the shine of a metal

INDEX

Anim

Migration

Brian Krumm

raintree

a Capstone company — publishers for children

Engage Literacy is published in the UK by Raintree.
Raintree is an imprint of Capstone Global Library Limited, a company
incorporated in England and Wales having its registered office at
264 Banbury Road, Oxford, OX2 7DY – Registered company number:
6695582

www.raintree.co.uk

Printed and bound in the United Kingdom.

Animal Migration

ISBN: 978 1 4747 1819 6

Image Credits

Dreamstime: Fishermancn, 20, Hanhanpeggy, 6; Minden Pictures: BIA/Jan Wegener, 28, Flip Nicklin,
15, Ingo Arndt, 29; Newscom: Arco Images/picture alliance/H. Reinhard, 31, Photoshot/Oceans-Image/
Michael Patrick O'Neill, 18, Visual&Written/Mark Conlin, 19; Shutterstock: Alfie Photography, 5, Ana
Gram, 27, Arena Photo UK, 17 (top), Arto Hakola, back cover, BMJ, 30, Chantal de Bruijne, cover (bottom
right), Chris G. Walker, 12, EcoPrint, 22, Erwin Niemand, 4, Ethan Daniels, 14, Galyna Andrushko, 9,
Jerome Whittingham, 24, melissaf84, cover (left), Perry Correll, 10, Richard Whitcombe, 17 (bottom left),
Robert Hardholt, 23, suebmtl, cover (top right), 11, Vadim Petrakov, 1, Vilainecrevette, 17 (bottom right);
U.S. Fish and Wildlife Service: George Gentry, 7, Linda Welch, 25
Design and Map Elements by Shutterstock

Contents

Migrating animals

Every year, birds fly from one part of the world to another. Fish swim across oceans. Animals move from east to west or north to south and across any type of land that you can imagine. Each year, many different kinds

of animals travel to places that are far away. This is called animal *migration*. It is the action animals take to move from one area to another at different times of the year.

Animals migrate for many reasons. The *resources* they need to survive, like food or water, change during the year. As seasons change, fewer resources are near them, and more resources can be found far away. Animals must move to where they can find food and water.

Animals also have a better chance of finding a partner or giving birth somewhere safe if they migrate. The animals must travel to new areas. They sometimes travel thousands of kilometres as part of their journey.

Fact: Many animals eat a lot of food before they migrate. This gives them the energy, or strength they need, for the long trip.

There are other important reasons why animals migrate. Some animals migrate to other areas during the winter for food and warmer weather.

Scientists have watched animals make their journeys for many years. And they have learned a lot. They learned that the most important reason why animals migrate is that they must travel to new places to survive. The animals will continue to migrate as long as they walk, swim or fly on the Earth.

Scientists also learned that many of these animals have the *instinct* to find their way. The animals weren't taught or told where they need to go. Instead, they can find their way as they travel. Animals are born knowing how to do this.

Animals migrate to find food and to leave dry or cold weather. Migration is needed for both the animal and its young to survive. Keep reading to learn about different types of animals that migrate.

Finding out what went wrong

Scientists closely watch how animals migrate to find out how healthy or unhealthy a place is. Animals move between healthy areas when they travel. Sometimes things can go wrong. For example, birds can get ill or die from dirty air or cold weather. When fewer birds migrate than in the past, there could be a serious problem for scientists to study.

Monarch butterflies

People love monarch butterflies. They enjoy seeing the orange and black butterflies fly through the air. At the end of each summer, people can watch monarch butterflies migrate. The butterflies travel thousands of kilometres from the countries of Canada and the United States. Many fly to a small area in the country of Mexico that butterflies have gone to for thousands of years.

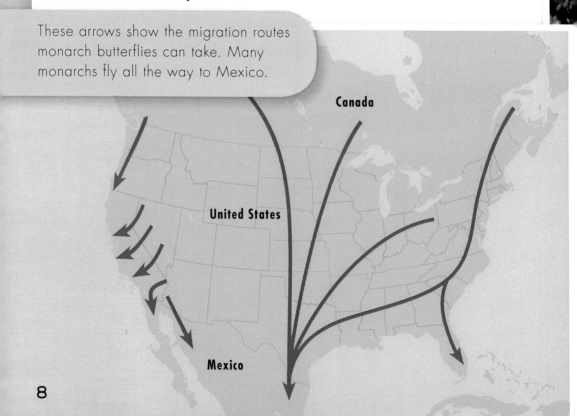

These arrows show the migration routes monarch butterflies can take. Many monarchs fly all the way to Mexico.

Canada

United States

Mexico

8

Millions of butterflies fly to a mountain area in Mexico. There, more than 10,000 butterflies can gather in one tree. The number of butterflies can cause tree branches to bend and even break.

Fact: The distance between London and New York City, USA, is about the same distance the monarch butterflies take as they migrate. That is almost 4,800 kilometres.

monarch butterflies

The butterflies stay in Mexico during the autumn and winter. In March, the female butterflies lay eggs. Then the new butterflies begin to fly north. It takes a few *generations* of butterflies to make the entire trip back. A generation is made up of a group of butterflies born at the same time. The butterflies lay eggs as part of each generation. The last grouping finally makes it back to the United States or Canada. When summer ends, the monarchs will make the journey south.

Monarchs and milkweed

Monarch butterflies use the *milkweed* plant for food. The butterflies also lay their eggs on it. Some people in the United States plant milkweed in their gardens to help the butterflies.

This monarch can be tracked as it migrates.

Scientists have a way to track, or follow, monarchs. A light sticker can be placed on a butterfly's wing. The sticker often has a number, a phone number, and an e-mail address on it. People can use this information to tell the place and date the butterfly was found. Many butterflies are found dead along the way to Mexico. But many are found that have made the trip all the way to Mexico.

Humpback whales

Whales are huge *mammals*, or warm-blooded animals, that live in the sea. Humpback whales make sounds like cries. Scientists think the whales make these sounds to communicate and to find partners. These sounds travel very long distances and can be heard for many kilometres in the oceans.

Humpback whales can jump up from the water's surface.

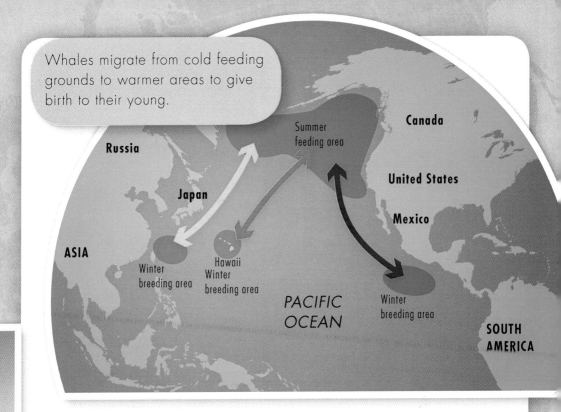

Whales migrate from cold feeding grounds to warmer areas to give birth to their young.

Russia

Japan

ASIA

Winter breeding area

Hawaii Winter breeding area

Summer feeding area

Canada

United States

Mexico

PACIFIC OCEAN

Winter breeding area

SOUTH AMERICA

The whales are also known for their amazing migrations. They travel thousands of kilometres from icy waters at the top of the Earth. This is where the whales feed during the summer. The places they travel to during the winter are close to the middle of the Earth. This is where they have their young. The trip is amazing because the whales have to cover a long distance, and they are very large. These gentle giants are as long as a minibus and as heavy as 20 cars.

Humpback whales travel thousands of kilometres to have young. The whales can be found each winter near the countries of Japan and Mexico or the US state of Hawaii. At these places, the whales find partners to make young, give birth, and feed their young. This all happens before the whales return to their summer feeding grounds in the north.

This mother humpback whale travels with her young.

Tracking migration

People can track animals in many ways. These different ways include putting fin *tags* on sea animals and leg bands on birds. Scientists have used tags that can be tracked by machines that circle the Earth in space. These machines give scientists information that can be used to understand patterns like how far an animal can travel in a day. The scientist shown in the photo is about to tag a humpback whale. By tracking the animals, scientists have learned that humpback whales travel about 5 to 11 kilometres per hour when they migrate. They also learned that the whales take very few breaks.

Leatherback sea turtles

Sixteen thousand kilometres is a very long distance to swim! That's about the same distance between the countries of England and Australia. Imagine travelling thousands of kilometres every year underwater! Leatherback sea turtles migrate this distance each year. They cross ocean water in the Earth's warmer areas to look for jellyfish to eat. Then they travel south to make young.

This map shows the migration routes the Pacific leatherback sea turtles take.

Russia

PACIFIC OCEAN

United States
California

China

Indonesia

SOUTH AMERICA

PACIFIC OCEAN

The leatherback sea turtle does not have a hard outer shell. The turtle has a pink spot on its head. Scientists think this spot lets light in, which tells the turtle when to migrate.

Plastic or jellyfish?

Sea turtles sometimes think plastic bags and other plastic floating in the sea are jellyfish. The turtles then feed on these things. The plastic stays in their stomachs and can kill the turtles.

17

Leatherback sea turtles have been on the Earth for millions of years. They are the largest type of sea turtle in the world. They can grow to be more than 2 metres long and can weigh as much as 900 kilograms.

Fact: Leatherback sea turtles can weigh almost as much as a small car.

These sea turtles are *endangered* animals, so they may die out. One reason why is because turtles are caught in fishing gear while out at sea. This is dangerous because

the turtles can die or be badly hurt. There are other reasons why leatherback sea turtles may die out. Places they live are often damaged, and people sometimes take their eggs for food.

Scientists have tagged turtles in many locations. They use objects in space to track the turtles' migration routes. Hopefully, the results from the studies will help more turtles survive. For example, the studies can help fishing companies keep out of the areas where sea turtles travel. People are also working to protect the places where the turtles live.

Wildebeests

More than one million wildebeests migrate in Africa. The migration is an amazing sight to see. The animals travel from their living places to find plants to eat. Wildebeests usually live in the plains of southeastern Africa. A plain is a large, flat area with few trees. The animals migrate at the end of the rainy season. The wildebeests know a dry season is beginning, so they go in search of food.

wildebeests

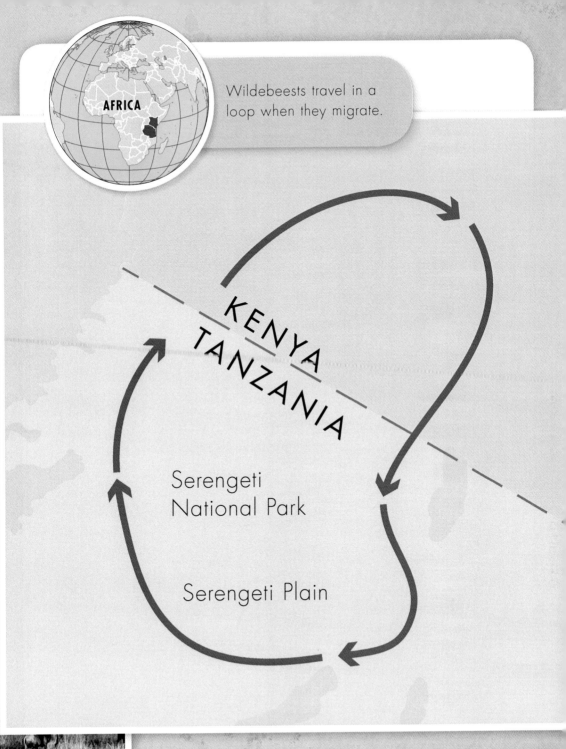

AFRICA

Wildebeests travel in a loop when they migrate.

KENYA

TANZANIA

Serengeti National Park

Serengeti Plain

Migration for the wildebeests can be very dangerous because *predators* that hunt the animals for food are along the route. The migrating wildebeests must cross a river as part of their trip. The river is filled with giant crocodiles. The crocodiles hunt the wildebeests.

Crocodiles aren't the only danger to the wildebeests. Some wildebeests drown while trying to cross deep or fast-moving river water. Scientists have recorded about 5,000 wildebeest deaths in a single location. But for all the thousands of wildebeests that die, many more live to continue the trip.

Zebra migration

Zebras also migrate in Africa. Hundreds of thousands of zebras migrate alongside the wildebeests. The animals must keep away from predators, which include the crocodiles in the rivers they cross.

Arctic terns

The tiny arctic tern makes the longest migration of any animal on the Earth. Arctic terns weigh about as much as a mobile phone. They travel from the top of the Earth to the bottom of the Earth each year. Each bird travels around 64,000 kilometres round trip!

arctic tern

Fact: Arctic terns can live more than 30 years, so they fly many kilometres during their lives. A lifetime of migrations is about the same as three trips to the Moon and back.

Scientists tag arctic terns and can use information that is tracked by an electronic system to learn how the birds migrate. They found that arctic terns follow routes that are full of twists and turns instead of flying in a straight line. The birds may follow these patterns to keep from flying right into the wind, which could hold them back. They also follow strong winds to help them migrate.

This arctic tern has a tag on its leg, so it can be tracked.

tag

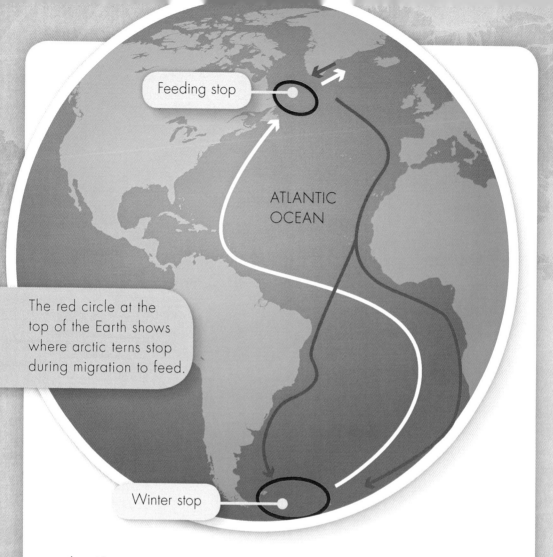

Feeding stop

ATLANTIC OCEAN

The red circle at the top of the Earth shows where arctic terns stop during migration to feed.

Winter stop

Arctic terns start at the top of the Earth and travel as far as the bottom of the Earth. This is where arctic terns come together during the winter. Many female birds then go back to where they were born to have babies.

Unlike other migrating animals, arctic terns take a break during their trip. They spend about a month in the North Atlantic Ocean. Scientists think they fill up with food during the break. It is much harder to find food in the cold waters of the south than in the north.

geese

Birds on the move

When people think about migration, many imagine birds flying south in a V-shape. Arctic terns don't migrate like this, but many other birds do. The shape helps the birds save energy. Each bird flies slightly above the bird behind it. As the bird flaps its wings, it helps the bird behind it by giving that bird a little lift.

More migrations

Many more animals in the world migrate each year. They test their own strength and will to survive along the way. Many migrating animals die during the journey. But migration continues, and scientists watch the patterns.

Another migrating animal is the banded stilt. This bird in Australia travels more than 1,600 kilometres in two days. That is almost the same distance as the distance between London and Naples in Italy. Banded stilts fly from areas on the coasts to lakes formed by heavy rains. Once they are there, the birds find partners and have their young. The birds leave once the lakes become dry.

banded stilt

ROAD CLOSED
RED CRAB MIGRATION
NO ENTRY BY VEHICLES
BEYOND THIS POINT

Christmas Island red crabs

Bright red crabs take over Christmas Island near Australia each October. They come from forests to the seashores to find partners and lay eggs. The pavements and streets on the island turn bright red because of the crabs.

caribou

Caribou in North America, bats in Africa, and penguins in Antarctica migrate, too. Hundreds of different kinds of birds migrate in countries and areas all over the world.

Migration is needed for life to continue on the Earth. In the air, in water and on land, migrating animals can be found everywhere. The migration patterns are amazing and so are the animals. Which one of these animals would you like to learn more about?

emperor penguins

Glossary

endangered in danger of dying out

generation group of people or animals born around the same time

instinct behaviour that is natural rather than learned

mammal warm-blooded animal that breathes air; mammals have hair or fur; female mammals feed milk to their young

migration act of moving from one area or country to another

milkweed plant with milky juice and pointed pods; monarch butterflies lay eggs only on milkweed

predator animal that hunts other animals for food

resource something useful or valuable to an animal or person

route road or course followed to get somewhere

tag label that is attached to something or someone in order to identify it

Index